Who Was
Rachel Carson?

Who Was
Rachel Carson?

by Sarah Fabiny

illustrated by Dede Putra

Penguin Workshop

To Emma, Bailey, and Celia:
may you all find your calling—SF

PENGUIN WORKSHOP
An Imprint of Penguin Random House LLC, New York

Text copyright © 2014 by Sarah Fabiny.
Illustrations copyright © 2014 by Penguin Random House LLC. All rights reserved.
Published by Penguin Workshop, an imprint of Penguin Random House LLC, New York.
PENGUIN and PENGUIN WORKSHOP are trademarks of Penguin Books Ltd.
WHO HQ & Design is a registered trademark of Penguin Random House LLC.
Manufactured in China.

Visit us online at www.penguinrandomhouse.com.

Library of Congress Control Number: 2014952922

ISBN 9780448479590   10 9 8 7 6 5 4 3 2

Part of the *What Is Science & Technology?* Boxed Set, ISBN 9780593090138

Contents

Who Was
Rachel Carson?

As a little girl, Rachel Carson liked to sit on
the porch of her family's farmhouse and hold her
mother's conch shell to her ear. As she pressed the

seashell to her ear, Rachel looked out at the fields and woods that surrounded her home. Rachel loved the plants, the animals, and even the insects that lived in the fields and woods. But the magical sounds that seemed to come from deep inside the shell made her dream of the sea. More than anything, Rachel wanted to stand on the shore of the ocean. She wanted to feel the waves wash over her feet.

Rachel was a shy girl, but she was also determined. Not only did she dream of the sea, she also dreamed of being a writer. Rachel knew that if she worked hard and held on to her dreams that maybe someday they might come true. And that's exactly what happened. Even though Rachel faced many challenges in her life, through her hard work and determination she became a writer—a writer who knew all about the sea, the shore, and all the creatures that made their homes there.

In her books, Rachel explained scientific ideas about nature in a way that ordinary people could understand. She also showed how all living things are connected. Rachel wanted people to understand how important it is to look after the planet we share with every plant, insect, and animal.

When she sat on her family's porch holding the shell to her ear, little did Rachel know that her dream would one day help shape the world we all live in.

Chapter 1
Creatures Great and Small

Rachel Carson was born in Springdale, Pennsylvania, on May 27, 1907. Her mother, Maria McLean, was the daughter of a Presbyterian minister. She had been a schoolteacher who also gave private piano lessons. Maria was forced to give up her job when she married Robert Carson, since married women were not allowed to teach in Pennsylvania at the time.

Rachel's father, Robert, owned sixty-five acres of farmland and woods in Springdale, a town about fifteen miles north of Pittsburgh, near the Allegheny River. The property included a small two-story house, a barn, outhouses, a chicken coop, and a springhouse.

The Carsons kept a few pigs, horses, cows, and chickens. By the time Rachel was born, she already had two older siblings—a sister, Marian, and a brother, Robert Jr.

Rachel and her dog, Candy, spent a lot of time exploring the land that surrounded their home. The woods and fields were full of all kinds of plants, animals, and insects, and Rachel was fascinated by all of them. Rachel's brother and sister were much older, so Rachel spent a lot of time alone. But she didn't mind, as she considered all the creatures her friends. She watched birds making their nests, butterflies flitting through the grass, and fish swimming in the streams.

Although the rushing water of the streams made Rachel happy, her biggest dream was to see the ocean. Rachel's mother had a conch shell, and Rachel loved holding it to her ear. She would pretend she could hear the ocean's waves rushing up and down the beach.

Rachel's mother was an avid bird-watcher. She also believed it was important for young people to study nature. Mrs. Carson taught Rachel that people must share the world with other creatures

and be respectful of them. She would watch as her
mother carried insects out of the house. Rachel's
mother didn't even own a flyswatter!

Rachel and her mother would take long walks in the fields and woods. When Rachel had questions about the things they saw, her mother would answer them. If she wasn't able to answer Rachel's question, she would show Rachel how to find the answer in books about science and nature.

Rachel actually persuaded her brother to stop hunting rabbits on the family's property, because they reminded her of the characters in the Beatrix Potter books her mother read to her.

Rachel started school in the fall of 1913. She loved school and learning, but she spent many days at home. If the weather was too cold, Rachel stayed at home and was taught by her mother. If other children in the class were ill, Mrs. Carson didn't want to take the chance of Rachel getting sick. Even though Rachel missed a lot of school, she was usually an A student. Mrs. Carson was an excellent teacher; she had been a schoolteacher, after all.

Chapter 2
A Writer Is Born

Rachel's favorite books were *The Wind in the Willows* and the Peter Rabbit books. They were stories about animals and how animals live in nature. Rachel loved reading, and she pleaded with her father to let her go with him when he went into town so that she could visit the library. Soon she started writing her own stories about animals and the wonder of nature.

Each month a magazine called *St. Nicholas* came in the mail for Rachel. It was a publication for children that was filled with stories and poems

from writers such as Mark Twain and Louisa
May Alcott and illustrations by artists such as
Norman Rockwell. Rachel's favorite section of
the magazine was called the St. Nicholas League.

It sponsored contests and printed articles, stories,
and drawings that had been submitted by
children. Winners were awarded gold badges,
and silver badges were given to runners-up.

Children who had won silver *and* gold badges became honor members. They received cash prizes.

When Rachel was ten, she decided it was time to send one of her stories to *St. Nicholas* magazine. She thought that maybe her work was good enough to win a prize. Rachel wasn't sure what she wanted to write about, but she got an idea from her brother, Robert. At the time, Robert was a soldier in the US Army fighting in World War I. In one of his letters home, he told the family about a Canadian pilot. The pilot had kept his plane flying even after one of the wings had been shot off.

Rachel worked very hard on her story and finally sent it off to the magazine. Then she waited to hear back from them. On a September morning in 1918, Rachel received the latest issue of the magazine. There in the St. Nicholas League section was her story, "A Battle in the Clouds." Underneath the title was her name, and under that were the words "Silver Badge."

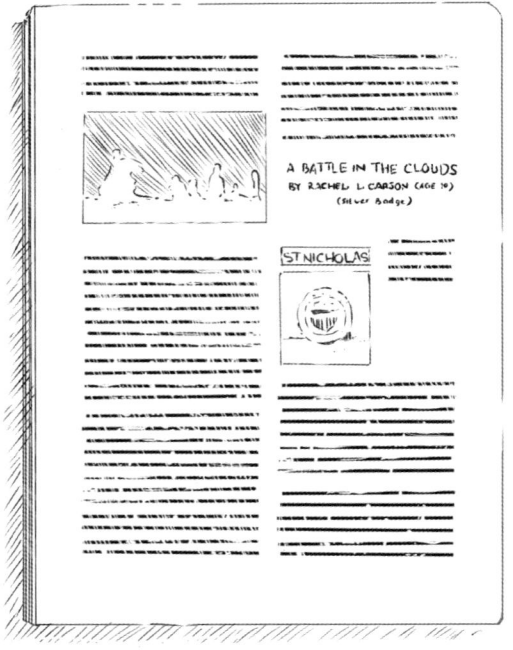

Winning the silver-badge prize was exciting for Rachel. It inspired her to write more stories. Most of them were about World War I. In February 1919, Rachel received a gold badge from the magazine for one of her stories. Because Rachel had won a silver and a gold badge, she also got a cash prize. The prize was ten dollars, which was a lot of money at the time. Rachel began to think that maybe she could be a real writer someday.

And that day would come much sooner than Rachel had ever imagined. She had written an essay about why she liked *St. Nicholas* magazine for her eighth-grade English class, and the magazine bought her essay to use in its advertising! They paid Rachel a penny a word, which came to a little over three dollars. This money was a payment and not a prize. Later Rachel would say that she "became a professional writer at the age of eleven." She even wrote

"first payment" on the envelope that the check
came in and never threw it out.

Rachel continued to write stories when she
entered high school. She also worked hard to get
good grades so that she would be able to attend
college. And Rachel was determined to go to
college.

Rachel liked spending time on her own and writing with no one else around. Because she was a serious student, teachers were happy to have her in their classes. But Rachel was shy.

ST. NICHOLAS MAGAZINE

    THE MAN WHO STARTED *ST. NICHOLAS* MAGAZINE,
DR. JOSIAH GILBERT HOLLAND, WANTED "A
MAGAZINE FOR CHILDREN, A MAGAZINE OF LIVELY,
WELL-WRITTEN STORIES, POETRY, AND ARTICLES."
MARY MAPES DODGE, A CHILDREN'S BOOK AUTHOR,
WAS CHOSEN TO BE THE EDITOR AND OVERSEE
THE MAGAZINE. BECAUSE SHE WAS AN AUTHOR
HERSELF, SHE SAW THE MAGAZINE AS A "CHILD'S
PLAYGROUND; WHERE CHILDREN COULD BE
DELIGHTED AS WELL AS BE IN CHARGE." THE
MAGAZINE WAS FIRST PUBLISHED IN 1873, AND
THE LAST ISSUE WAS PUBLISHED NEARLY SEVENTY
YEARS LATER, IN 1940. THE MAGAZINE INCLUDED
WORK BY FAMOUS AUTHORS SUCH AS ROBERT

LOUIS STEVENSON, EMILY DICKINSON, AND LAURA
INGALLS WILDER. IT ALSO HELPED WRITERS
AND POETS LIKE F. SCOTT FITZGERALD, WILLIAM
FAULKNER, AND E. E. CUMMINGS GET THEIR START.

MARY MAPES DODGE

Some of her classmates thought she was a teacher's
pet. Rachel decided to join the field hockey team
in high school so that she would make friends.

She liked being outdoors on the hockey field, and
she liked being on a team, too. She also played
basketball and cheered at pep rallies for the high-
school football team.

Even though Rachel enjoyed sports and her new friends, schoolwork was still the most important thing to her. Her classmates wrote a poem about her and put it beside her picture in the high-school yearbook:

> *Rachel's like the mid-day sun*
> *Always very bright.*
> *Never stops her studying*
> *'Til she gets it right.*

Rachel graduated top of her class in high school. It was now time for her to get ready to leave home and set off on a new adventure—college!

Chapter 3
Choosing a Path

Rachel started college in the fall of 1925, during the middle of the "roaring twenties." It was only a sixteen-mile car ride from Springdale to Pennsylvania College for Women, but it was like another world for Rachel.

Rachel's mother had wanted her daughter to study at an all-girls school that was close to home. Mrs. Carson thought Pennsylvania College for Women, in Pittsburgh, would be the perfect place. Rachel was happy to go along with her mother's choice, but the cost of the first year of college would be a thousand dollars, and the Carsons did not have that much money to spend on Rachel's education. Fortunately, the dean at the college wanted Rachel to come and study there, so the school gave her a scholarship. They also helped Rachel get a loan that covered the rest of her

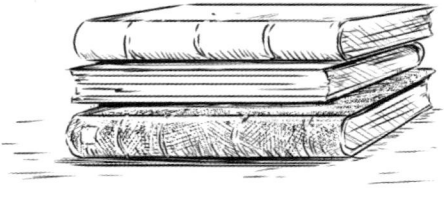 tuition, as well as room and board and all of Rachel's books.

College was a new challenge for shy Rachel. She didn't have as much money as a lot of her classmates did. She didn't have fancy clothes like they had. And Rachel couldn't afford to go to the

movies or go get a soda with them. (She had even borrowed a Model T Ford to make the trip from Springdale!) It must have been hard for Rachel not to be able to join her classmates when they went out. But she always reminded herself that she was at college to learn and not to play.

Because she wanted to be a writer, Rachel decided to study English literature and composition at college. Rachel's English teacher was Miss Grace Croff. She quickly became Rachel's favorite teacher. And Rachel soon became one of Miss Croff's favorite students. She admired Rachel's determination and saw that Rachel had real talent.

But English literature and composition classes weren't the only ones that Rachel had to take at college. For her music requirement, Rachel decided to play the violin. And in her second year at Pennsylvania College for Women, Rachel had to take a science course. She chose biology,

which is the study of plant and animal life.
Although she loved nature, Rachel didn't really
want to take a science course, because her science
classes in high school had been dull and boring.

However, Miss Mary Skinker's biology class changed Rachel's mind about studying science. Miss Skinker had the same passion for the natural world as Rachel did. And Rachel was thrilled when the biology classes

MARY SKINKER

included field trips to nearby state parks.

On one trip Miss Skinker had all the students split apart layers of rock with hammers and chisels. Rachel hit a piece of dull, gray rock. When the piece broke open, what a surprise she found! Inside the rock was a fossil of a fish that had swum in an ancient ocean. Miss Skinker explained that this dry, rocky area near the college had been at the bottom of an ocean a very long time ago.

Rachel also loved finding out about how living things moved and breathed and ate. As part of her class, she had to dissect animals. The class cut open and looked at grasshoppers, frogs, and starfish.

While some of the students thought it was a messy job, it fascinated Rachel. She was learning how the wildlife she loved lived and grew.

Miss Skinker's biology class excited Rachel so much that she decided to take more science classes.

Her main interest was zoology, which is the study of animal life. And it was the animals that lived in the sea that fascinated Rachel the most.

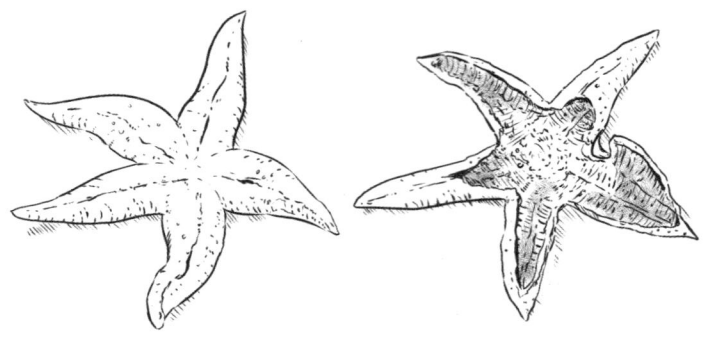

Rachel's grades in English classes were excellent, and she loved learning from Miss Croff. But Rachel also loved science classes. She had to make a decision and choose between studying English or science. Rachel worried that if she switched to studying science, she would miss English classes and writing. And if she focused on English, Rachel would no longer have Miss Skinker teaching her about the beauty of the natural world.

One night while she was sitting in her dorm room, Rachel took a book of poetry off her shelf. As a storm blew outside, she opened the book to a poem called "Locksley Hall." The main character in the poem had to make a hard decision, just like Rachel. One line in the poem jumped out at Rachel as she sat on her bed, listened to the storm, and tried to decide what to do. The line was, "For the mighty wind arises, roaring seaward, and I go."

A WOMAN'S PLACE

WOMEN HAD WON THE RIGHT TO VOTE IN 1920.
AND IN THE MID-1920S IT WASN'T UNUSUAL FOR
YOUNG WOMEN TO ATTEND COLLEGE. BY 1928
WOMEN EARNED 39 PERCENT OF THE COLLEGE
DEGREES AWARDED IN THE UNITED STATES. BUT
EVEN THOUGH WOMEN ATTENDED COLLEGE AT
THAT TIME, IT WASN'T COMMON FOR THEM TO FIND
WORK ONCE THEY GRADUATED. MEN DOMINATED
THE PROFESSIONAL WORLD, WHILE WOMEN—EVEN
COLLEGE GRADUATES—WERE STILL EXPECTED TO
REMAIN AT HOME, BUSY AS WIVES AND MOTHERS.

The words stuck in Rachel's head. She read them over and over again. At that point Rachel was convinced that somehow her life would be connected to the sea as well. She decided that she would choose a life as a scientist rather than a life as a writer.

Chapter 4
Dreaming Big

Rachel's classmates thought she was making a big mistake. As a young woman in the 1920s it would be much easier to find a job as a writer than as a scientist. But once Rachel made up her mind about something, she was determined to make it happen. Rachel studied hard in school for the next two years. She also worked on the school paper and played on the hockey team.

In the spring of her last year at Pennsylvania College for Women, Rachel applied to Johns Hopkins University as a graduate student. She wanted to continue her studies in science. Johns Hopkins University was a very famous school. Not only did Johns Hopkins accept Rachel because of her excellent grades, they also awarded her a scholarship! Rachel was excited and relieved. Getting the scholarship meant that her family wouldn't need to worry about finding the money to pay for her tuition.

Rachel was also invited to spend that summer at the Marine Biological Laboratory at Woods Hole, in Massachusetts. Woods Hole was a very famous research laboratory. Rachel would get to work with well-known scientists and explore sea life—it was everything she had been dreaming of.

The summer at Woods Hole was more than
Rachel had hoped for. For the first time she got
to experience the power and beauty of the ocean
that she had only ever read about. During the six
weeks at Woods Hole, Rachel worked in the lab,
walked along the seashore, and made friends. She
knew that this was the life that she wanted.

That fall on her way to Johns Hopkins University in Baltimore, Maryland, Rachel stopped at the US Bureau of Fisheries in Washington, DC. She wanted to find out what she should study to get a job as a biologist. Rachel spoke with Mr. Elmer Higgins, the acting director. He explained the types of jobs that were available at the Bureau of Fisheries. He also told her that they had never hired a woman scientist.

This made Rachel more determined than ever to find a job working as a scientist.

There were very few women in Rachel's graduate program at Johns Hopkins University. And it wasn't always easy to keep up with her work. Classes started right after breakfast and went on until after dinner, so there wasn't a lot of free time to study.

After three tough years, Rachel received her master's degree on June 14, 1932. Unfortunately, the country was in the middle of the Great Depression.

So many people were out of a job. At that time
it was difficult for scientists to find work, but
being a woman scientist made it even harder.

No one wanted to hire a woman biologist. After a lot of looking, Rachel finally got a job as a teacher at the University of Maryland. It wasn't exactly what she wanted to do, but she was lucky to have a job during such a difficult time. With the money she made she was able to help the members of her family who were struggling because of the Depression.

In 1935, Rachel's father died. It was a sad time for the Carson family, and it also made life difficult for Rachel's mother. Rachel decided she needed to find a better job to help her family. So Rachel went to talk to Elmer Higgins again. Mr. Higgins told her there were no jobs available for biologists at the Bureau of Fisheries. But Mr. Higgins did need someone to help rewrite scripts for an educational radio program. The program was called *Romance Under the Waters*.

The scripts were filled with long, fancy scientific words that didn't always make sense to the audience. Mr. Higgins wanted the listeners to enjoy the radio program, and to learn from it, so he asked Rachel to make the stories easier to understand. Rachel had never written a script before. She was nervous about taking the job, but she knew that her talent as a writer and her knowledge of the underwater world were just what was needed.

JOHNS HOPKINS UNIVERSITY

JOHNS HOPKINS UNIVERSITY, IN BALTIMORE, MARYLAND, IS NAMED AFTER A SUCCESSFUL BUSINESSMAN WHO HAD MADE HIS FORTUNE FROM THE RAILROADS. WHEN HE DIED IN 1873 HE LEFT $7 MILLION IN HIS WILL TO BUILD A UNIVERSITY AND HOSPITAL. AT THE TIME IT WAS THE LARGEST PHILANTHROPIC (DONATED) GIFT IN US HISTORY. THE UNIVERSITY WAS FOUNDED ON JANUARY 22, 1876. AT FIRST ONLY MEN WERE ALLOWED TO ATTEND. WOMEN WERE ADMITTED TO THE GRADUATE SCHOOLS STARTING IN THE 1880S.

BUT IT WASN'T UNTIL NEARLY ONE HUNDRED
YEARS LATER, IN 1970, THAT WOMEN WERE
ALLOWED TO STUDY AS UNDERGRADUATES AT THE
UNIVERSITY. JOHNS HOPKINS UNIVERSITY IS
STILL KNOWN AS ONE OF THE FINEST RESEARCH
SCHOOLS IN THE WORLD.

Chapter 5
Never Give Up

It was the perfect job for Rachel, and the weekly broadcasts soon became a huge success.

Not long after she started, Rachel was asked by Mr. Higgins if she would like to write an introduction to a booklet about fish. Rachel jumped at the chance. She stayed up late writing the piece. She wanted it to be perfect. When Rachel showed the introduction, "The World of Waters," to Mr. Higgins the next day, he shook his head.

Rachel was surprised. What could be wrong with it? Rachel's boss told her that the introduction was *too* good! He told her it should be published in a magazine, not in a government booklet.

Although Rachel loved her job, she still wasn't making enough money to really help her family. She started writing articles for magazines and newspapers to earn extra money. All this work meant Rachel didn't have much free time,

and she was tired a lot. But she was doing what she loved—writing about nature.

Rachel decided to try to sell the piece her boss had called "too good." She did some more work on "The World of Waters" and sent it to *The*

Atlantic Monthly, an important magazine that was known for recognizing new writers. They agreed to publish it if Rachel made some changes and gave it a new title, "Undersea." When the article appeared in the magazine, Rachel showed it to Mr. Higgins. Once again, Mr. Higgins shook his head. Now what could be wrong with it, Rachel wondered. This time Mr. Higgins said it should be an entire book and not just a magazine article!

Rachel's boss wasn't the only one who thought her work should be more than an article in a magazine. Quincy Howe, an editor at Simon & Schuster Publishing Company, and Willem van Loon, a famous naturalist, both wrote to Rachel. They persuaded Rachel to turn her article into a book.

Because Rachel was a perfectionist, and because she was also working full-time, it took her three years to finish her first book. But in 1941,

Under the Sea-Wind was published. Her book was filled with stories and interesting facts about the creatures that lived in the sea. It also showed how their lives were all connected. Rachel used words that someone who wasn't a scientist could easily understand and enjoy.

Rachel's book received excellent reviews, but it didn't sell well. One month after *Under the Sea-Wind* was published,  the United States entered World War II. Suddenly the country was at war, and people were worried about how their lives would change. No one was interested in reading a book about sea life and the ocean.

Rachel was upset that even though the book got good reviews, very few people bought and read it. She even told a friend, "Don't ever write a book," because she was so discouraged by the lack of sales for *Under the Sea-Wind*.

The Fish and Wildlife Service (the new name for the Bureau of Fisheries) was very busy during the war. They moved their offices from Washington, DC, to Chicago in the spring of 1942 and hired Rachel to work on the *Food from the Sea* series. War rationing meant that people were eating more fish and less meat. The *Food from the Sea* bulletins were a way to teach people about different kinds of fish.

In the spring of 1943, the Fish and Wildlife Service moved back to Washington, DC, and Rachel moved to a house in Silver Spring, Maryland.

Rachel's mother, brother, sister, and nieces all depended on her and lived with her at various times throughout her life. So, although she had just been promoted, it was difficult for Rachel to support herself and all the members of her family. She continued to write magazine articles in addition to her job at the Fish and Wildlife Service.

WORLD WAR II AND RATIONING

WORLD WAR II, ALSO KNOWN AS THE SECOND GREAT WAR, WAS A GLOBAL WAR THAT LASTED FROM 1939 TO 1945. MUCH OF THE WORLD, INCLUDING MOST OF EUROPE AND ASIA, WAS INVOLVED FROM THE VERY START. BUT THE UNITED STATES DIDN'T ENTER THE WAR UNTIL 1941, WHEN THE JAPANESE BOMBED PEARL HARBOR, A US NAVAL STATION IN HAWAII. BECAUSE OF THE WAR, MANY PRODUCTS WERE IN SHORT SUPPLY— EVERYTHING FROM METAL AND RUBBER TO MEAT AND BUTTER. BY 1945, MANY OF THESE PRODUCTS HAD BEEN RATIONED, MEANING THAT FAMILIES WERE ONLY ALLOWED TO BUY A CERTAIN AMOUNT EACH WEEK, USING GOVERNMENT-ISSUED RATION STAMPS.

5   OBA AORM B 2153   A

5   UNITED STATES OF AMERICA   5
OFFICE OF PRICE ADMINISTRATION

RATION COUPON
FOR
FIVE
POINTS
MEAT, FATS, FISH, and CHEESES

5   OBA AORM B-2153   A   5

UNITED STATES OF AMERICA

The events of World War II gave Rachel plenty of ideas. There was much research done about radar during the war. It inspired Rachel to write an article about bats and how their sonar skills are like radar. The article was called "The Bat Knew It First." The US Navy recruiting office called it "one of the clearest expositions of radar yet made available for public  consumption." As always, Rachel wanted the science of the natural world to make sense to everyone.

The atomic bombs that were dropped on Hiroshima and Nagasaki in Japan in August 1945 ended World War II.

It was a relief that the war was over. Maybe life could go back to normal. But those powerful bombs made a lot of people, including Rachel, realize that the destruction could have a very bad impact on the entire planet.

Rachel wanted everyone to understand
that people—and the decisions
they made—had a big effect on the
environment and every other living thing.
The earth had to be protected.

Chapter 6
Success at Last

Rachel spent a lot of time with the people she worked with at the Fish and Wildlife Service,

including her good friend and coworker Shirley Briggs. They went hiking and bird watching together. They went to parties and enjoyed their free time.

But Rachel still worked as hard as ever. And
over the next few years she had some amazing
experiences. She went
deep-sea diving. Seeing
sharks, octopuses, and
other sea creatures up close
was one of the greatest
moments of her life.

Afterward, she told a friend, "Everything seems a little different." She also tracked alligators in the swampy Florida Everglades and spent time on a research boat in the North Atlantic Ocean.

All the fantastic experiences she had and the discoveries she made went into her next book, *The Sea Around Us*. The book was published in 1951. In it, Rachel taught people how the oceans affect all of us.

The way Rachel wrote in this book was almost like poetry. Her words were gentle, and she expressed her ideas in a clear and thoughtful way. Rachel talked about "ecology," which is the relationship between a group of living things and their environment. It was the first time most people had heard this word, and Rachel wanted her readers to understand how important it was.

The Sea Around Us became a huge best seller, and Rachel earned a good deal of money from the book. During the Christmas season of 1951, four thousand copies of the book were being sold every day.

The book, published by Oxford University Press, won two special awards—the 1952 National Book Award for Nonfiction and a Burroughs Medal in nature writing. It stayed on the *New York Times* best-seller list for eighty-six weeks, and it was translated into twenty-eight languages.

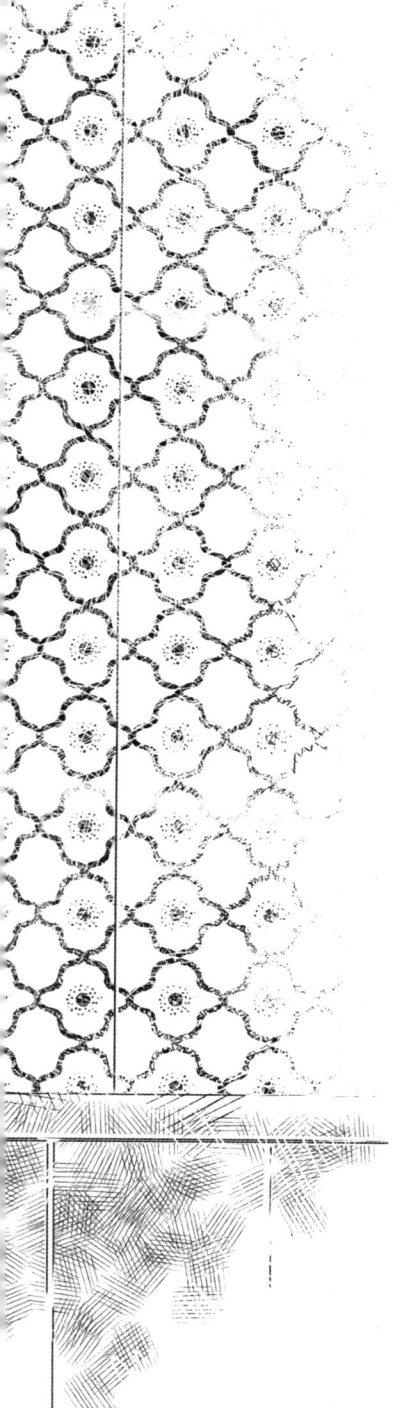

Readers were fascinated by Rachel's knowledge and love of the sea. Many people wanted to meet her and ask her about her latest book. But this was hard for the shy Rachel Carson. She found it very difficult to live with the fame that her incredible book had brought.

With the huge success of *The Sea Around Us*, Rachel decided to get her first book, *Under the Sea-Wind*, printed again. This time the book became a top seller. People were interested in what Rachel had to say. Now she had two books on the best-seller list.

Her money worries were finally over. In 1952
Rachel quit her job and devoted her time to
writing. And what she wanted to write about was
the natural world that she loved so much.

Rachel decided to research new ideas for
her next book. She and her mother drove up
and down the East Coast of the United States,
studying the coastal shores and taking notes.
Rachel bragged that she and her mother drove over
two thousand miles in just a few months. They
visited coral beaches in Florida, sandy beaches
in North Carolina, and rocky beaches in Maine.

Rachel wanted to observe the plants and sea life in those very different kinds of places.

Now that she was writing full-time, Rachel was able to finish her next book much more quickly. In October 1955, *The Edge of the Sea* was published. Readers were excited to read Rachel's new book.

It became an instant best seller. Like her
other books, she used poetic words to describe
the animals she had seen on the beaches.
She explained how all the animals in these
places had adapted to the places they lived.

Whether they lived on gentle coral beaches, warm sandy beaches, or rough rocky beaches, animals and plants became what they were because of their environment. Rachel also helped readers understand how they fit into those environments, too.

With the success of her third book, Rachel became even more famous. Her fans wanted to meet her. They tracked her down when she was getting her hair done in a beauty parlor. They came up to her when she was trying to have a quiet meal in a restaurant. They even knocked on her hotel room door early in the morning. Rachel was happy that so many people read and liked her books, but it was sometimes difficult for her to handle all the attention. She was still the same shy girl from Springdale, Pennsylvania, who liked exploring the woods on her own.

THE POETRY OF RACHEL CARSON

RACHEL CARSON BECAME KNOWN FOR HELPING PEOPLE UNDERSTAND SCIENCE THROUGH THE USE OF BEAUTIFUL AND POETIC WORDS. HER WRITING MADE IT EASY FOR PEOPLE TO UNDERSTAND DIFFICULT IDEAS.

HERE SHE WRITES ABOUT BARNACLES IN *THE EDGE OF THE SEA*:

"THE BARNACLES FURL THEIR NETS AND SWING SHUT THE TWIN DOORS THAT EXCLUDE THE DRYING AIR AND HOLD WITHIN THE MOISTURE OF THE SEA."

AND ON STARFISH HUNTING IN A KELP "FOREST":

"HERE AND THERE A STARFISH, HAVING INVADED THE FOREST FROM BELOW ON THE PREVIOUS HIGH TIDE AND INCAUTIOUSLY LINGERED, STILL CLASPS

A MUSSEL WITHIN ITS SINUOUS ARMS, GRIPPING THE SHELLS WITH THE SUCKER-TIPPED ENDS OF SCORES OF SLENDER TUBE FEET."

Chapter 7
Battling On

While doing her research for *The Edge of the Sea*, Rachel had read lots of articles and books. Much of what she read had to do with the effect of pollution on our world. Rachel became concerned about how cities and factories across the country were dumping garbage and industrial waste into rivers and oceans.

Rachel was sad about how the ocean she loved so
much was being used as a giant trash can. She also
read about strong chemicals called "pesticides"
that were being sprayed on crops. Farmers and big
corporations claimed they needed the pesticides
to kill insects and animals that damaged plants
and crops. Even the US government made
announcements that they had to wage war on the
pests that were a threat to food crops. But Rachel
knew that this would be terrible for plants and
animals—and humans who ate them.

In 1957, Rachel's niece, Marjorie, the daughter of her sister, Marian, had died from pneumonia, and Rachel was now looking after her niece's young son, Roger, in addition to her own eighty-nine-year-old mother. Rachel loved her family, but taking care of them took a lot of energy.

And Rachel herself was not always in good health. She was often tired and weak from surgery she had had many years earlier. But none of that stopped her from reading and writing and researching. More than anything she wanted the world to hear about the things she discovered.

Despite all the demands on her time, Rachel was looking for a new project. She was thinking about how she could tell the world all the things she was learning about pollution and pesticides. And then she received a letter from a friend, Olga Owens Huckins. The letter described how Olga had found numerous dead robins in her yard. She said that the birds had died because of pesticide spraying that had been done to control mosquitoes. And yet there were still more mosquitoes than ever!

The pesticide that had been sprayed was called DDT. Olga asked Rachel if she could do something about it. Rachel knew that she definitely could.

In 1953 she had bought a piece of land on the coast of Maine and built a small cottage. Her books had made her famous, and Rachel longed for a place to escape to. Rachel brought Roger to live there with her and her mother. During the day, Rachel and Roger wandered along the seashore and explored nature. They studied moss and ferns.

And at night they took a flashlight and watched
the sea life in the rock pools—small crabs,
starfish, and anemones. It was just the kind of
peace and quiet Rachel needed. It reminded her of
her childhood and exploring her family's farm in
Pennsylvania. Rachel wanted to teach Roger about
the wonders and beauty of nature, just like her
mother had taught her.

Rachel decided to spend more time learning about pesticides and their effect on nature. She knew that it was not going to be an easy research project. A lot of people told her it was a bad idea, but Rachel knew someone had to speak up.

The more research Rachel did, the more upset she became. She was discovering how pollution and pesticides threatened birds, insects, fish, and other animals. And what about human beings? If pollution and pesticides made animals sick, surely they would make people sick, as well.

DDT

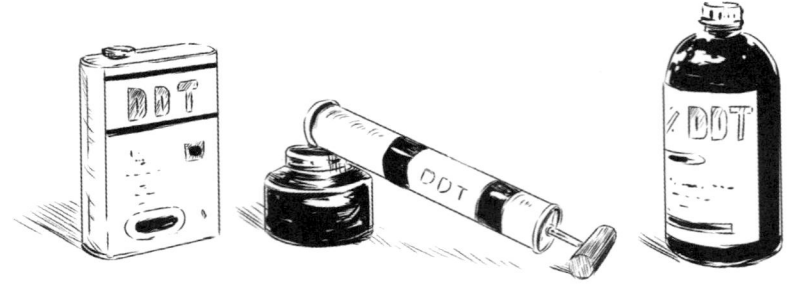

    DDT, OR DICHLORO-DIPHENYL-TRICHLOROETHANE,
HAD BEEN USED DURING WORLD WAR II TO KILL
LICE AND OTHER INSECTS THAT CARRIED DISEASES.
AFTER THE WAR, THE US GOVERNMENT ALLOWED
A CHEMICAL COMPANY CALLED DUPONT TO SELL IT
TO CONSUMERS AND BUSINESSES, EVEN THOUGH
SCIENTISTS WERE WORRIED ABOUT WHAT EFFECT
IT MIGHT HAVE ON THE ENVIRONMENT. THE US
GOVERNMENT CONTINUED TO USE IT TO CONTROL
PESTS. FARMERS USED IT TO KILL BUGS AND
RODENTS THAT RUINED THEIR CROPS. THE US
GOVERNMENT AND THE DUPONT COMPANY TOLD
AMERICANS THAT THE CHEMICALS WERE SAFE. BUT
MORE SCIENTISTS WERE DOING RESEARCH ON
THESE CHEMICALS. THEY DISCOVERED THAT THEY
DID MORE HARM THAN GOOD TO THE ENVIRONMENT.
THESE CHEMICALS WERE POISON AND WERE
MAKING PEOPLE, PLANTS, AND ANIMALS SICK.

Rachel spoke to lots of people—experts on insects and animals, friends she used to work with in the government, doctors who treated people with diseases, and even hunting and fishing groups.

It was dangerous work, and some of Rachel's friends worried about her. They thought that if Rachel criticized big business, government agencies, and farmers that used pesticides, these groups might try to ruin her reputation. But Rachel didn't have any connection to business, and she no longer worked for the government. She hoped that this would allow her to do her research more freely. She wanted to show people that keeping the air and water clean was important, even necessary.

Rachel kept this new work a secret. She wanted to make sure that no one would try to stop her. As always, because Rachel wanted to make sure her research was absolutely perfect, she checked

and double-checked facts. She asked scientists to read her work to be absolutely certain that it was accurate. She also asked everyone to help her keep her project a secret.

The problem with pesticides and pollution was worse than Rachel had thought. Most people thought the government would protect them from dangers and wouldn't do anything to make them sick. But Rachel's research showed her that this wasn't true.

Chapter 8
Silent Spring, Noisy Spring

In November 1958, right in the middle of Rachel's research into DDT and other pesticides, her mother had a stroke. Within a few days, Maria Carson died. Rachel was so sad that she stopped working. Her world wasn't the same without her mother.

On top of that, Rachel seemed to have one illness after another. First she got the flu, then a bad stomach ulcer, and then arthritis. Rachel also suffered infections in her knees, which meant that she wasn't able to go for walks along the seashore for months. In 1960, Rachel received even worse medical news: She was diagnosed with cancer. She was very sick. Would she ever be able to finish work on her project?

But Rachel knew that her work was
important. The world needed to know about
it, so she kept writing. She was often in pain
and she was in and out of the hospital a lot.

Early in 1962, Rachel's latest book was ready. Rachel and her agent, Marie Rodell, discussed titles like *The War Against Nature* and *At War with Nature*. Although the subject of the book was serious, those titles sounded too harsh for Rachel's poetic writing. Marie suggested *Silent Spring* as a title. Rachel had included a chapter in her book about how pollution and chemicals had an effect on birds, everything from sparrows to bald eagles. She had thought about using "Silent Spring" as the title for that chapter. But Rachel's agent thought the title would work for the whole book.

MARIE RODELL

It would let people know that the future of the earth would be silent and sad if something wasn't done to stop the use of pesticides and pollution.

CHAIN OF DESTRUCTION

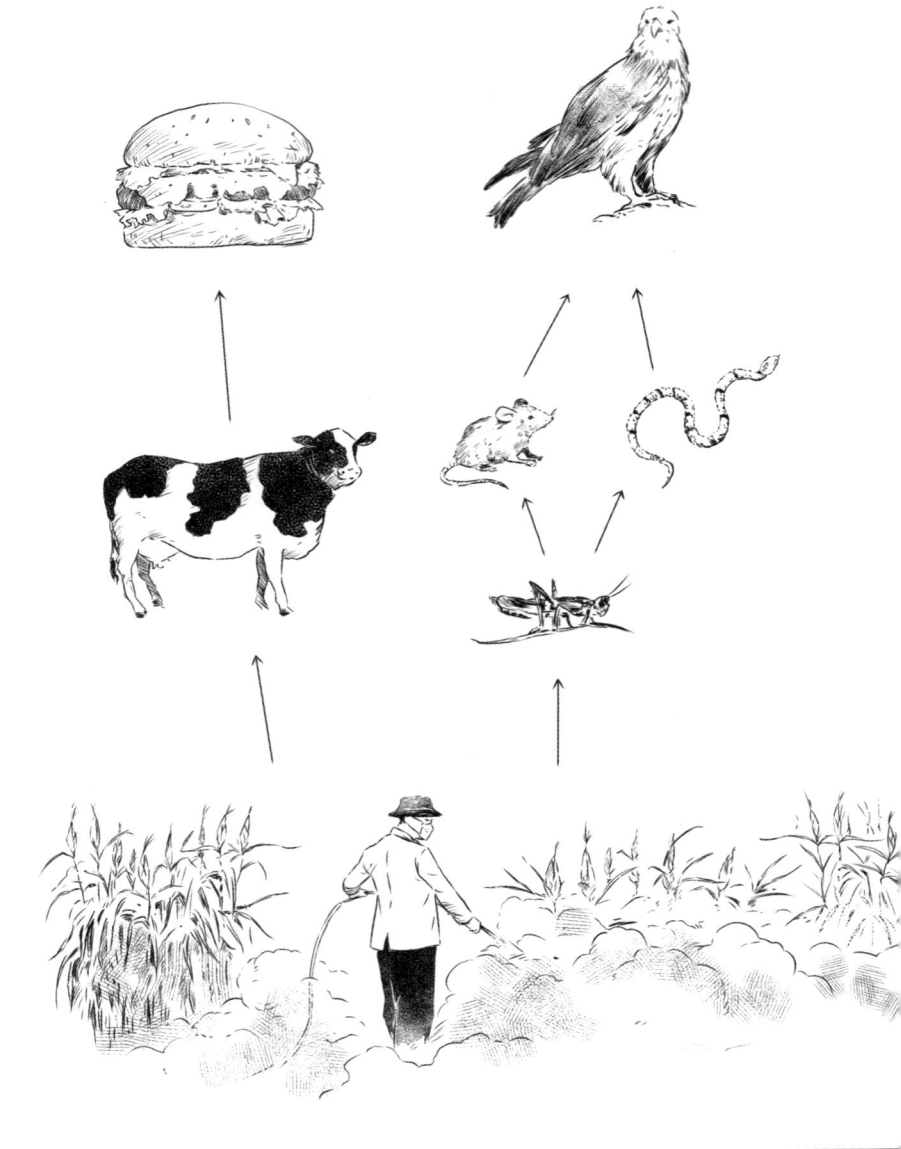

RACHEL CARSON EXPLAINED HOW THE USE OF PESTICIDES AND CHEMICALS CREATES A CHAIN OF DESTRUCTION. WHEN POISONOUS PESTICIDES AND CHEMICALS ARE SPRAYED ON CROPS AND PLANTS, THE PESTICIDES REMAIN INSIDE THE BODIES OF ANIMALS AND INSECTS THAT EAT THE PLANTS. BIRDS AND RODENTS THEN EAT THE INSECTS AND PLANT CROPS. LARGER ANIMALS EAT THE BIRDS AND RODENTS. AND FINALLY HUMANS EAT THE POISONED PLANTS AND ANIMALS. THE PESTICIDES AND CHEMICALS HAVE FOUND THEIR WAY INTO ALMOST EVERY LIVING THING.

Rachel had put a lot of hard work into her book. She had written and rewritten her words so that readers would understand the complicated scientific ideas. It had taken her over four years to complete *Silent Spring*. But would people read the book and see it as a warning? Would people listen and want to help change things?

Marie Rodell sent *Silent Spring* to Rachel's publisher. She also sent it to *The New Yorker* magazine. A few days later, Rachel's phone rang late at night. The editor of *The New Yorker,* William Shawn, had just finished reading the book. He called Rachel as soon as he finished it.

WILLIAM SHAWN

He was shocked by the things Rachel had written about. How could the government allow big chemical companies to harm plants, animals, and humans? Was it too late to stop the damage?

Those words were music to Rachel's ears. It was exactly the kind of reaction she wanted. And she hoped that everyone who read the book would have the same reaction. Mr. Shawn asked if he could run parts of Rachel's book in his magazine before the book was published. Rachel said yes.

Although Rachel had received fan mail in the past, it was nothing like the amount she was receiving now. As soon as chapters of *Silent Spring* appeared in *The New Yorker*, letters started pouring in. People were shocked by what Rachel had to say.

A few of the letters said that Rachel didn't know what she was talking about. But most of the letters were very supportive. An article in *The New York Times* newspaper said that Rachel had written a story "few will read without a chill, no matter how hot the weather." But Rachel and *The New Yorker* weren't the only ones to get letters. Concerned and outraged readers also sent letters to newspapers, chemical companies, and the government.

Representatives from the chemical companies and the Department of Agriculture weren't happy with what Rachel had said in her book. They decided to fight back. They wrote newspaper and magazine articles and went on TV and the radio saying that Rachel had gotten her facts wrong.

Pesticides Industry Up in Arms

But Rachel was sure that her research would stand up. She had always worked hard to make sure that whatever she wrote was true. And Rachel didn't want to completely ban the use of pesticides. She just wanted people to learn more about them and to understand that they had an effect on the total environment—everything found in nature could be harmed by pesticides. Rachel wanted the government and the chemical companies to make sure they tested the chemicals before they used and sold them.

Chapter 9
Peace and Quiet

Awards and invitations to speak flooded in.
Although Rachel was still shy about speaking
in public, she wanted to reach as many people as
possible. She agreed to be on TV since millions
of people would get to hear her and listen to
what she had to say. On April 3, 1963, *CBS
Reports* broadcast a one-hour TV program
called "The Silent Spring of Rachel Carson."

CBS wanted people to hear Rachel's message, even though chemical companies urged CBS not to broadcast the program and had even threatened to cancel their advertising. The show was seen by over ten million people. It reached many who hadn't read Rachel's book and weren't aware of the pollution and pesticide issues.

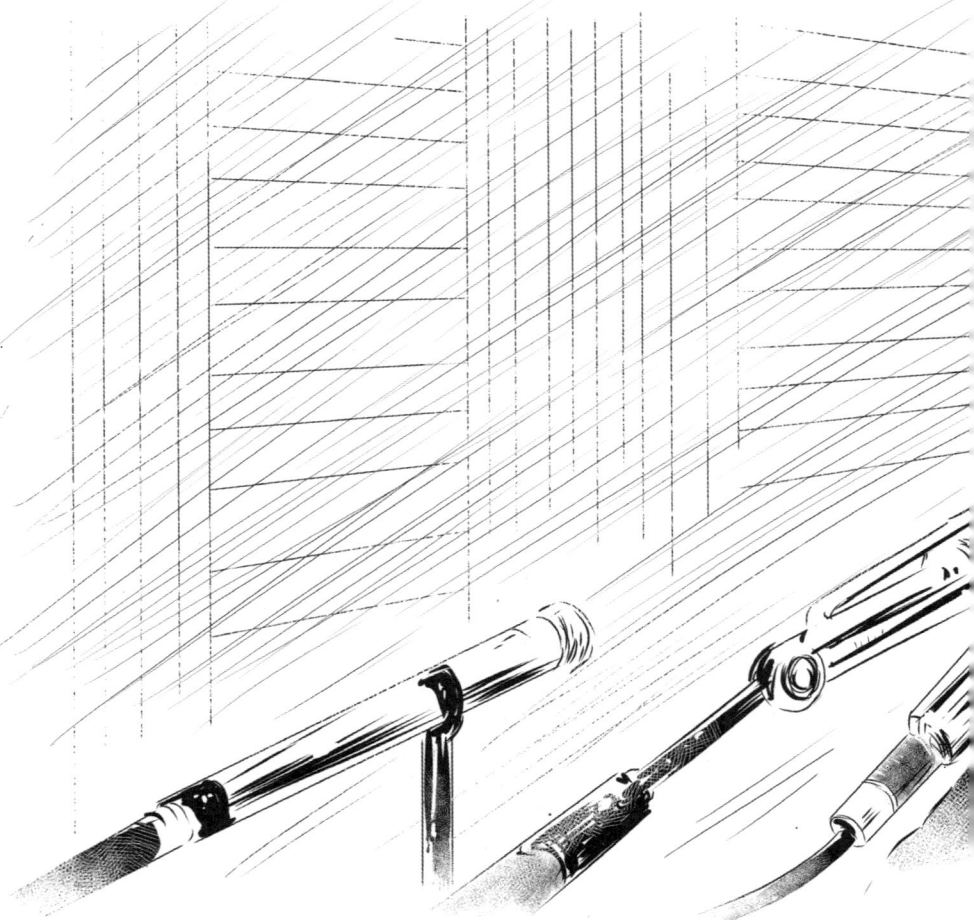

Even the president of the United States, John F. Kennedy, had read Rachel's work. He also heard about the people who disagreed with her. President Kennedy asked some scientists to do a special report that would help them decide who was right. On May 15, 1963, the president's special committee report was released.

The report said that Rachel's facts were correct. Because of that report, new laws were passed that limited chemical pollution and the use of pesticides. The government also followed Rachel's suggestions about how to find other ways to control insects that damaged crops.

Rachel was becoming more and more famous, but she was also getting weaker because of her cancer. In the summer of 1963, Rachel decided she needed a break from all the attention. She went to her house in Maine to spend time with her friends. She wanted to listen to the sound of the sea and watch the creatures along the shore. Being close to the ocean reminded her of exactly why she had dedicated her life to looking after nature.

Even though Rachel had escaped to Maine, she did her best to speak to as many people as she could. Invitations poured in from around the world. But her cancer continued to spread.

During one speech, Rachel was so weak that she had to speak from the podium while sitting in a wheelchair.

Rachel returned to Maryland early in 1964. She was tired, but she was proud and excited that her book had captured people's attention. People in the United States and around the world were talking about the danger of pollution and pesticides. Laws were being passed that would slow down the damage that people were doing to the world. The years of hard work had paid off. The shy girl from Springdale, Pennsylvania, had made a difference.

On April 14, 1964, Rachel Carson died at her home in Silver Spring, Maryland. She was only fifty-six years old.

Since *Silent Spring* was published, it has become one of the most talked-about books in modern history. Rachel Carson opened the world's eyes to environmental issues that were too important to ignore.

AN IMPORTANT LEGACY

IT'S HARD TO CALCULATE RACHEL CARSON'S IMPACT ON THE LAWS THAT PROTECT OUR ENVIRONMENT. SHE WAS JUST ONE PERSON, BUT AS A PIONEERING ENVIRONMENTALIST, SHE CHANGED OUR COUNTRY—AND THE WORLD— FOR THE BETTER FOR GENERATIONS TO COME:

*   BETWEEN 1963 AND 1974, CONGRESS ENACTED SEVERAL POLICIES INCLUDING THE CLEAN AIR ACT, THE CLEAN WATER ACT, AND THE SAFE DRINKING WATER ACT.

- IN 1969, CONGRESS APPROVED THE NATIONAL ENVIRONMENTAL POLICY ACT, WHICH REQUIRED FEDERAL AGENCIES TO CONSIDER THE IMPACT OF MAJOR PROJECTS SUCH AS THE BUILDING OF ROADS AND DAMS, FOREST CLEARING, AND THE DRAINING OF MARSHLAND.

- IN 1970, PRESIDENT NIXON ESTABLISHED THE ENVIRONMENTAL PROTECTION AGENCY— A SINGLE AGENCY TO LOOK AFTER ALL THE GOVERNMENT'S ACTIVITIES THAT PROTECT THE ENVIRONMENT.

- IN 1972, DDT WAS BANNED FOR MOST USES IN THE UNITED STATES.

TIMELINE OF
RACHEL CARSON'S LIFE

1907	May 27, born in Springdale, Pennsylvania
1918	Publishes first story in *St. Nicholas* magazine
1925	Enrolls in Pennsylvania College for Women
1929	Gradates from college, spends summer at Woods Hole research laboratory
1932	Receives master's degree from Johns Hopkins University
1935	Starts work at Bureau of Fisheries; father dies
1941	Publishes first book, *Under the Sea-Wind*
1951	Publishes second book, *The Sea Around Us*
1952	Receives National Book Award for Nonfiction
1955	Publishes third book, *The Edge of the Sea*
1957	Adopts grandnephew, Roger, after the death of his mother
1958	Mother dies .
1962	Publishes *Silent Spring*
1963	Appears on *CBS Reports*
1964	Dies at the age of fifty-six

TIMELINE OF THE WORLD

World War I starts	1914
World War I ends; influenza epidemic kills an estimated 20–40 million people around the world	1918
Women win the right to vote	1920
Penicillin discovered	1928
US stock market crashes, setting off the Great Depression	1929
Scientists split the atom	1932
The Hobbit by J. R. R. Tolkien published	1937
World War II starts	1939
US drops atomic bombs on the Japanese cities of Hiroshima and Nagasaki; World War II ends	1945
The Diary of a Young Girl by Anne Frank published	1947
Dwight Eisenhower elected president of the United States, *Charlotte's Web* by E. B. White published	1952
Polio vaccine announced	1955
John F. Kennedy elected president of the United States	1960
Widespread use of DDT banned	1972

BIBLIOGRAPHY

Carson, Rachel. **Silent Spring**. Boston: Mariner Books, 2002.

* Kudlinski, Kathleen V. **Rachel Carson: Pioneer of Ecology**. New York: Puffin Books, 1989.

* Lawlor, Laurie. **Rachel Carson and Her Book That Changed the World**. New York: Holiday House, 2012.

* Levine, Ellen. **Up Close: Rachel Carson**. New York: Puffin Books, 2008.

Souder, William. **On a Farther Shore: The Life and Legacy of Rachel Carson**. New York: Crown Publishing, 2012.

* Venezia, Mike. **Rachel Carson: Clearing the Way for Environmental Protection**. Danbury, CT: Children's Press, 2010.

* Books for young readers